SACRED
PLACES

PHILEMON STURGES ILLUSTRATED BY GILES LAROCHE

⟨⟨⟨⟨

G. P. PUTNAM'S SONS

FROM THE BEGINNING OF HUMAN HISTORY, people everywhere have asked the questions: *Where did I come from? How should I live my life? What happens to me when I die?*

Many great thinkers, prophets, and teachers have found different answers. Their words and deeds have inspired others to believe in them, and the faithful have studied their teachings, written about them, and added their own insights. As a result, systems of belief, called religions, have developed. Each religion has its own symbols and its own way of doing things. But people of every religion have built sacred places where they go to worship, pray, study, and celebrate the great events in their lives and the lives of their holy people. Some are decorated with symbols or images made of sculpture, paint, colored glass, or patterned tile. Others speak with the quiet beauty of pure geometry.

There are many religions in the world, and most have many divisions within them. For simplicity's sake, Giles and I chose places sacred to people from five religions. This book is a celebration of the many different ways people have found to use the language of architecture to praise their Creator and to express their feelings about the mystery of life and death.

—P. S.

 THE HINDUS — Hinduism, which developed in India over the last thirty-five centuries, is the world's oldest living religion. It has a loosely organized structure, and creeds are a matter of each person's faith. Hindus share the belief that life is an endless cycle of being born, living, dying, and then being reborn in another form. This rebirth is called reincarnation. Since a person's behavior in this life will influence what or whom that person will become in the next, it is important to honor the gods, cooperate with one another, and respect all living things.

Hindus believe in one Creator in that they believe there is one great creative force. It is called Brahman. Brahman is all energy and power. There are countless Hindu gods and goddesses who, like everything else in this world, came from Brahman. The greatest of these are Brahma the creator, Vishnu the preserver, and Shiva the destroyer and re-creator.

Hindus usually worship at home, where a special place is set aside for prayer and meditation, but people go to temples or natural sacred sites to honor particular gods, pray for special intentions, or celebrate special events. The sacred word *om* (symbolized as) is recited during meditation by devout Hindus to bring them an awareness of Brahman.

Hindus have a rich literature of epic myths and written teachings such as the Vedas, the Bhagavad Gita, and the Upanishads.

Many other religions have emerged from Hinduism. One of these is Buddhism.

 THE BUDDHISTS — In about 600 B.C.E. (Before the Common Era), a young Hindu prince named Siddhartha Gautama gave up his power and money and left his family to live in poverty. He wanted to understand why there is so much pain in the world and learn how to be truly happy. While meditating under a tree, he suddenly understood and he became enlightened. He became the Buddha. Then he devoted the rest of his life to teaching people to alleviate suffering through meditation and enlightened living.

The Buddha taught that there are Three Universal Truths, Four Noble Truths, and the Eightfold Path (symbolized as ⊙) that one must follow to escape the endless cycling of life and achieve the great calm called nirvana. To follow the path is something you must do within yourself through prayer and meditation, but monks, who often live, study, and meditate in communities called *sanghas*, can help you.

After the Buddha's death, his teachings were written down; these are the *Pitakas* (rules for the *sanghas*), the Sutra (sayings of the Buddha), and the *Abhidharma* (underlying philosophy).

ABRAHAM'S GOD — Jews, Christians, and Muslims all believe that in about 2000 B.C.E. God spoke to a man named Abraham and said there is only one God. If Abraham loved God above all else, Abraham's children would become the fathers of great nations. According to Muslim tradition, Abraham took his eldest son, Ishmael, to a place in the desert, now called Mecca. There they built the first temple to the One God. It's called the Kaaba, and it still stands today.

Later, God asked Abraham to prove that he loved God above all else by sacrificing his son. (Jews and Christians believe this son to have been Isaac, Abraham's youngest son; some Muslims believe it was Ishmael.) So Abraham took him to the top of a hill called Mount Moriah. He bound him and laid him on a rock. As Abraham raised his knife, an angel stopped him and said he had proven his love and his son could live.

Isaac's children became the Jews, and later some Jews and many others became the Christians. The children of Ishmael became the Arabs, and then, even later, most Arabs and many others became Muslims. Followers of all three religions believe in the God of Abraham. They are often called "People of the Book."

 THE JEWS — In about 1250 B.C.E., God spoke to Moses, who was Isaac's descendant and the adopted son of the Pharaoh. God told Moses to leave the comfort of the Pharaoh's palace and lead the Jews from slavery back to the lands near Mount Moriah. On the way, atop a mountain, God gave Moses two stone tablets engraved with the Ten Commandments. Those words became the core of the five holy books dictated to Moses by God. Together they are called the Torah, which is the center of life for every Jew. As centuries passed, other prophets and holy people wrote other books that, together with the Torah and the songs of King David and King Solomon (the Psalms), became the sacred book Jews call the *Tanakh*.

The symbol is called the Star of David and has become a symbol of Judaism.

Jews believe that the most important things in this life are to study the Torah and do good works. They believe that they will live on after death as long as they are remembered in love (this is called *yizkor*), as they wait for the Messiah who will come someday to bring them into the presence of God.

THE CHRISTIANS — Around the year 30 C.E. (Common Era), a young Jew named Jesus came to Jerusalem. He said that he was the Son of God, the Messiah. He led a life of preacher, teacher, and healer, and tried to reform the Judaism of his time. Jesus was declared a heretic and was crucified on a cross (✝). When he died, his body was put in a tomb. Christians believe that he was resurrected from the dead before he

ascended into heaven. They also believe that all those who love Jesus will join him there and live forever.

The night before Jesus died, he had supper with twelve of his followers. He gave them bread and wine and asked that, whenever they gathered together, they do the same in order to remember him. This became a ritual known as the Eucharist, Communion, or the Lord's Supper.

Years later, the followers of Jesus wrote down his words. They're called the Gospels. These, together with many other writings of his early followers, are called the New Testament. The Christians combined this with the *Tanakh*, which they called the Old Testament, into one book, which they call the Bible. This book is central to Christian worship.

THE MUSLIMS — Muhammad was an Arab who became a skilled leader as well as a prophet. One night in about 610 C.E. he had a great vision while praying on the side of a mountain overlooking Mecca. The Angel Gabriel appeared and told him to recite the words of God that would be revealed to him from then on until he died. Throughout his life, Muhammad continued to have revelations, and these words were written down and compiled a few years after his death. These are believed by Muslims to be the actual words of God, and they call their sacred book the Koran.

Muhammad established five principles for Muslim worship. The first is to acknowledge that God is central to your life, that there is only one God, and that Muhammad is God's prophet. The second is to perform five daily prayers by facing the Kaaba and bowing and kneeling with your head to the ground. The third is to give generously to the needy. The fourth is to fast during the day for the month of Ramadan. The last is, if possible, to make the great pilgrimage to the Kaaba at least once in your lifetime.

Muslims believe that Muhammad, Jesus, Moses, and Abraham, as well as other prophets, were mortal men who became messengers of God, but Muhammad is the last and the greatest of the prophets. They also believe that all people who are virtuous, regardless of their religion, will join God in heaven in their next life.

The month of fasting, Ramadan, begins and ends when the first sliver of the new moon is sighted. The crescent moon ☽ is the symbol of Islam, which is the religion of Muslims.

CHARTRES CATHEDRAL
Chartres, France
1194–1260 • North tower and spire, 1507

This great Gothic cathedral dominates the town and the countryside around it. A cathedral houses the headquarters of a bishop, who, in some Christian denominations, is the head of all the churches in a district. It is usually the district's largest church. Chartres' north tower and spire and elaborately carved doorways are well known, and its stained-glass windows are considered to be among the most beautiful in the world.

People all over
the world have made
special places
where they gather
to worship,
celebrate, meditate,
and hope.

These are sacred places.

GREAT MOSQUE
Agadez, Niger • About 1500, rebuilt about 1845
A man chanting from the top of a tall tower called a minaret calls Muslims to prayer five times each day. A minaret stands next to their place of worship, a mosque. This minaret is made of mud bricks and palm tree beams.

UNITED CHURCH OF ACWORTH
Acworth, New Hampshire • 1820
Christians often ring a bell to gather people to their place of worship, a church. The bell hangs in a belfry, which is in a tower that is near or attached to the church. Here the belfry is in a tower over the front door. Sometimes, as in the north tower of Chartres, the tower is topped by a spire that some say points to heaven. Here it is capped with a small dome called a cupola, which symbolizes heaven.

PAGODA
Dali, Kunming, China • About 850
Pagodas are usually found near Buddhist temples. Like minarets, towers, cupolas, and spires, they rise above the physical world and call attention to the sacred place nearby.

The temple at Dali was destroyed long ago. This sixteen-tier tower is the largest of the three remaining pagodas.

They are places
where your
spirit sings and
your mind is filled
with wonder.

 SHRI MEENAKSHI AMMAN TEMPLE
Madurai, Tamil Nadu, India • About 1630
These are two of twelve great entrances to a large temple complex built to honor Parvati, the wife of the Hindu god Shiva. All together, these gateways resemble the towering Himalaya Mountains in the north. It's said that the temple buildings are covered with about thirty-three million images of gods, demons, and other creatures.

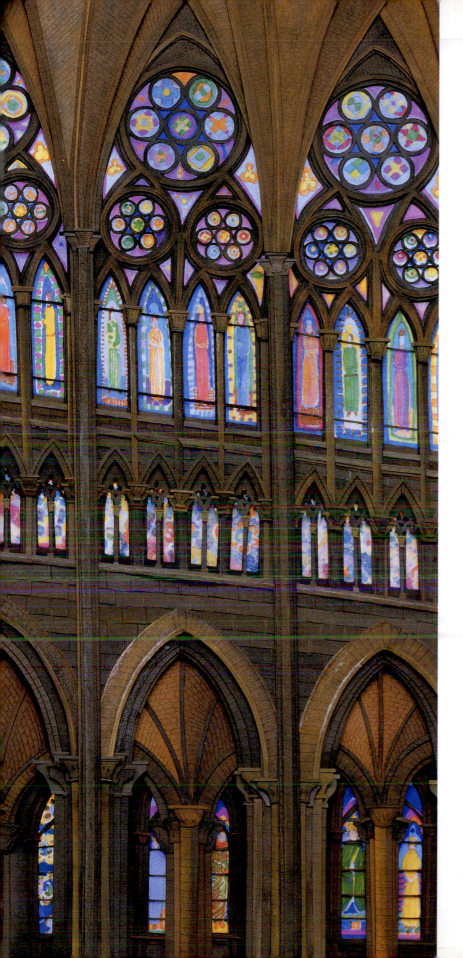

Some of these places took hundreds of years to build.

ABBEY CHURCH OF SAINT-DENIS
Saint-Denis, France • 270, 475, 630, 750,
1136–1147

In 270, a chapel was built over the tomb of Saint Denis, the first bishop of Paris. In 475, a large village church was built on the site. The church was dismantled and rebuilt in 630 and in 750. In 1136, work began on yet another church for the abbey, over the old chapel and tomb. This church is one of the first examples of Gothic architecture. It was expanded and restored over centuries, and is still being altered and restored today.

Elaborate ribbed stone arches support the roofs of Gothic churches, and the walls are made of stained-glass windows set between stone piers. These illustrate Bible stories, the life of Jesus, and the deeds of saints and martyrs. Some, like this great round window, are simply beautiful patterns of colored glass.

Some are hard to reach.

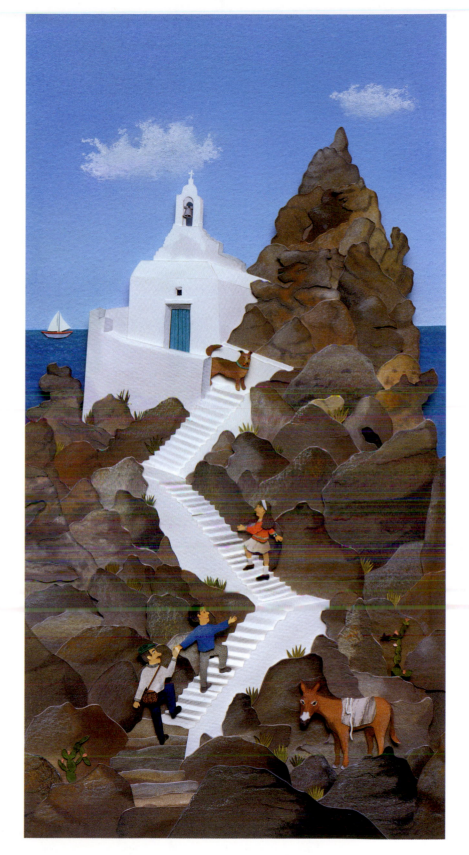

ABBEY CHURCH OF MONT SAINT-MICHEL

Near Avranches, France • The Abbey was begun in 1058 • The Abbey Church was completed in 1228

Abbeys, monasteries, and convents are places where Christians, usually monks or nuns, can practice their beliefs and pray for others while living in seclusion.

This abbey sits on a rocky island at the edge of the sea. Originally it could be reached only by boat or at low tide, but now a causeway connects it to the mainland.

Like Saint-Denis, Chartres Cathedral, and many other churches, the Abbey Church is built in the shape of the cross. The head of the cross faces east to greet the rising sun.

THE CHURCH OF AGIOS IOANNIS THEOLOGOS IN THE CLIFFS

Naxos, Greece • About 1600

This tiny chapel was built on the side of a steep hill on an island. To reach it, people must climb eight hundred feet up rocky paths and steep stairs. Some come here to leave an offering, ask for a special favor, or just watch the sun sparkling on the blue Aegean Sea.

Others are just down the street.

TEMPLE MICKVE ISRAEL
Savannah, Georgia • 1878

Nearly every neighborhood in the world has at least one place where people gather to worship together and to celebrate the important events in their lives.

This synagogue was built by the first Jewish congregation in Savannah. There are many other holy places in this neighborhood. The spire of the Wesley Monumental Methodist Church can be seen in the background.

And some aren't buildings at all.

GANGES RIVER GHAT

Varanasi, India • These steps have been built and rebuilt for over three millennia.

The waters of the Ganges River flow from the towering Himalaya Mountains and through the plains of northern India, bringing life, and sometimes destruction, to the land and people.

Many think that the Hindu god Shiva swam here, and they believe that if they do the same, their next life will be especially blessed. As many as a quarter of a million people come to the river here on a single day. Stairways, called ghats, were built to allow this throng of people to get to the water easily.

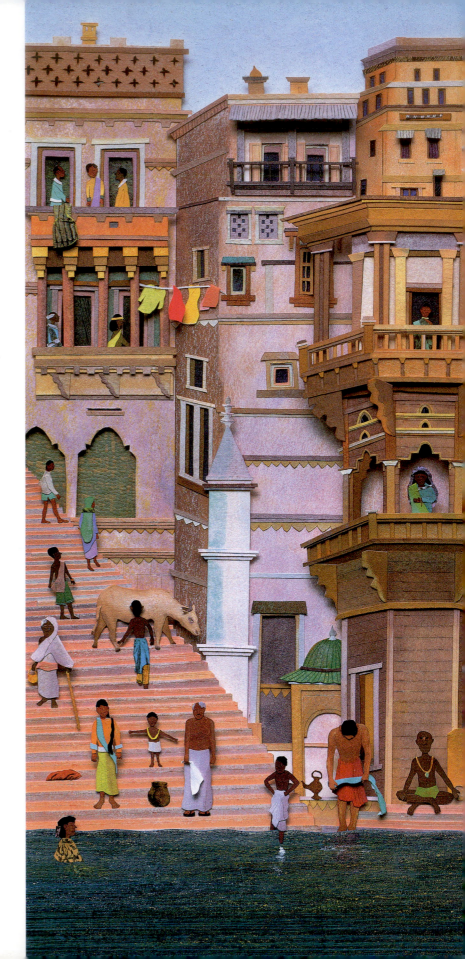

There are places people go to welcome those just born, or remember those who have died.

THE BAPTISTERY

Parma, Italy · About 1200

To become a Christian, a person is ceremonially washed and purified, either with a sprinkling of water or, in some Christian denominations, immersion. Adults can be baptized, and most Christian parents welcome their babies to their new life and religion by having them baptized as well. In some churches, the water is in a basin near the entrance to the church or in a deep pool at the front. Some churches have a special room called a baptistery for this ritual. In Parma, baptisms take place a separate building.

NEW ST. NICHOLAS CHURCH AND SPIRIT HOUSES

Eklutna Village, Alaska · 1954–1962

People of all religions believe that death is as important as birth and should be marked in a ceremonial way. Some people bury the bodies of their loved ones in the ground, some lay them to rest in special places called tombs, and some burn the bodies in a hot fire and then bury or scatter their ashes.

At this church, Native American and Christian customs blend. The bodies here are buried in the Christian tradition, but then spirit houses are built over the graves.

There are places like Jerusalem...

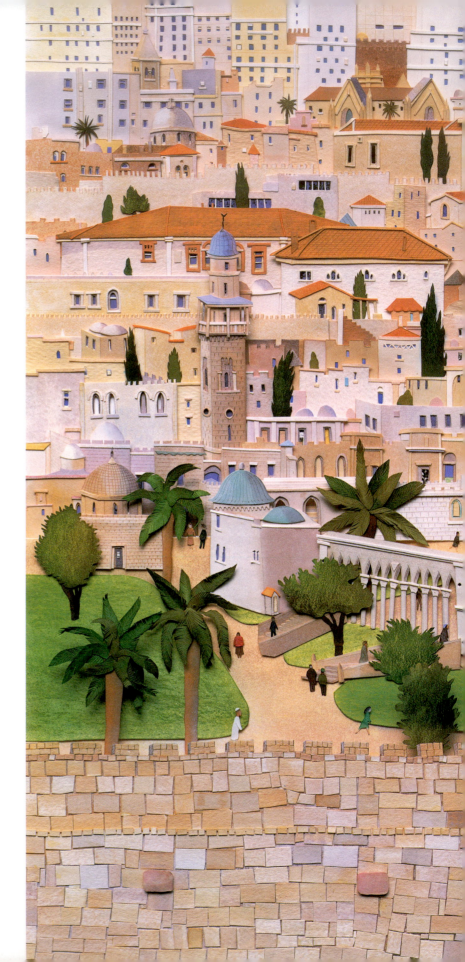

JERUSALEM
About 1000 B.C.E.
to the present

Jerusalem is sacred to Jews, Christians, and Muslims. In about 1000 B.C.E., King Solomon built the Jewish Temple on Mount Moriah. He built it over the rock where Abraham brought his son to be sacrificed, and he placed the Ark inside. The Ark was a special case that contained the stone tablets with the Ten Commandments and the original Torah. About five hundred years later the temple was destroyed by the Babylonians. Construction of the Second Temple began in 538 B.C.E., and in 20 B.C.E. King Herod expanded it with a splendid complex of buildings. Then, in 70 C.E., the Romans destroyed the Second Temple.

Shortly before the Second Temple's destruction, Jesus was crucified and buried in Jerusalem.

In 621 C.E., Muhammad had a vision in which an angel carried him from Mecca to Mount Moriah and back in one night. There he met Abraham, Moses, and Jesus. After they prayed together, Muhammad climbed a ladder into heaven, where he saw God.

The Dome of the Rock is in the foreground. The domes of the Church of the Holy Sepulcher can be seen to its left. The temple's Western Wall cannot be seen here, but would be on the far side of the Dome, to the left.

that are sacred to people with different religions.

THE WESTERN WALL OR WAILING WALL

About 20 B.C.E.

This is part of the western foundation wall that remained after the destruction of the Second Temple. It is called the Wailing Wall because Jews come here from around the world to weep and pray for their people. Many leave personal prayers on scraps of paper, which they put into cracks between its huge stones.

CHURCH OF THE HOLY SEPULCHER

335, 1048

The first Christian Roman emperor, Constantine, built the Church of the Holy Sepulcher over the tomb where Jesus was buried after his crucifixion. The original church was destroyed in war, but was rebuilt by the Crusaders when they captured Jerusalem about a thousand years ago. Shown here is the altar, where the ritual celebrating the Last Supper is performed.

DOME OF THE ROCK

685–691

This was built on the same site as the Jewish Second Temple. Muslims believe this is also the spot from where Muhammad ascended to heaven. The Dome of the Rock was built after Muhammad's death as a symbol of the unity of the three religions that worship the God of Abraham. The dome was originally covered with gold.

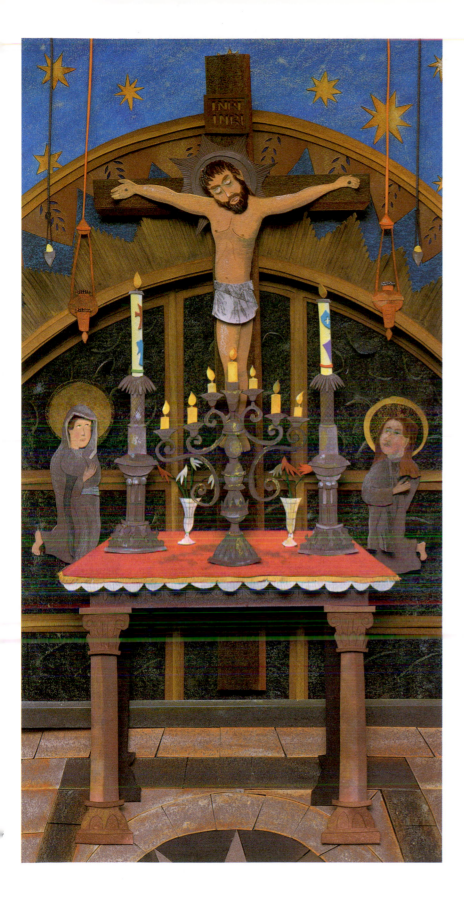

People have many different ways of worshiping in their sacred places.

 SELIMYE MOSQUE
Edirne, Turkey • About 1570
Friday is the Muslim holy day of the week, so each Friday, Muslims gather in a mosque for noontime prayers. Then their leader, an imam, stands halfway up a staircase called the *minbar*, reads from the Koran, and preaches. The arched niche, called the mihrab, faces Mecca so people know which way to face while praying.

 TEMPLE SOLOMON
Montreal, Canada • 1921
Saturday is the Jewish Sabbath, or holy day, so on that day they gather in their synagogues to worship. A cantor may sing sacred words, and then a designated passage for the week is read from the Torah by the rabbi or a member of the congregation. Sometimes the rabbi comments on the text. Then the cantor and the congregation sing psalms.

 MISSION SAN MIGUEL ARCÁNGEL
San Miguel, California
Mission founded in 1797 • Church built in 1816
Most Christians gather in a church on Sunday to pray and listen to a priest or a minister read from the Bible and preach from a pulpit, shown here. At certain services they may celebrate the Lord's Supper. Many churches have a special group of singers, called a choir, that leads the congregation in the singing of sacred songs called hymns.

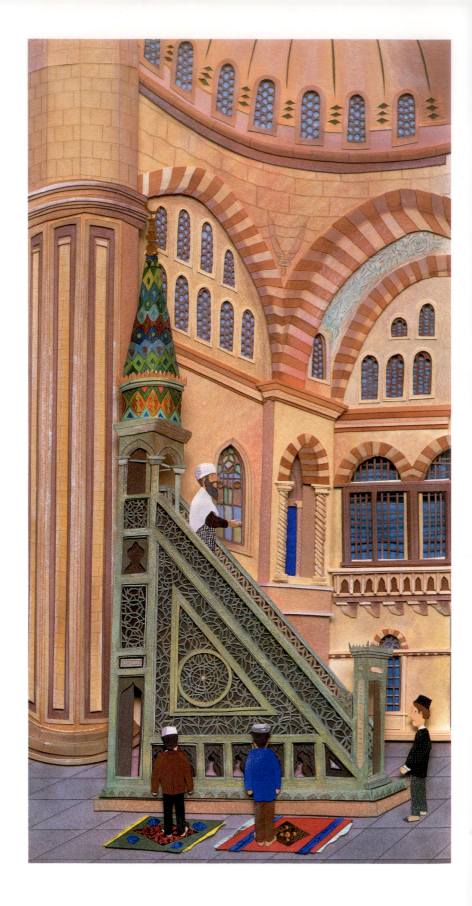

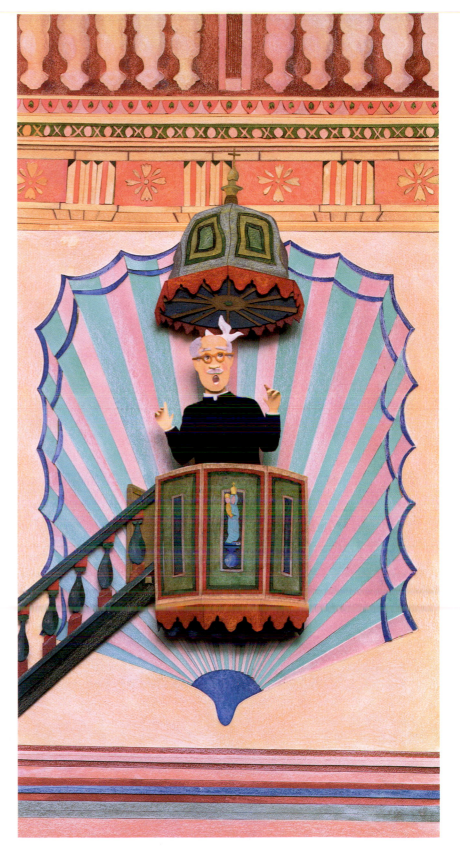

People come to this sacred place to pray and meditate.

 SOKKURAM GROTTO SHRINE
Kyongju, Korea • 751

Much of Buddhist worship involves quiet contemplation called meditation. Many *sanghas* have a temple or shrine with a statue of the Buddha where ordinary people as well as monks meditate, pray, and celebrate special occasions.

This statue of the Buddha rests in a grotto carved into the side of a mountain and is about ten feet high. He sits on a lotus petal and looks serenely out to sea.

People gather in these sacred places to worship with family and friends.

HENNIKER FRIENDS MEETING HOUSE
Henniker, New Hampshire • 1799

The Society of Friends, commonly called Quakers, does without formal ceremonies or preaching at its meetings. Every Sunday, its members gather together to sit quietly and pray. When someone feels moved, he or she stands up and says what's on his or her mind.

Quakers believe in conducting their lives with great simplicity, and their meeting houses reflect this.

THE HA'ARI SYNAGOGUE OF THE SEPHARDIM
Tsefat, Israel • Exact date unknown

This ancient synagogue stands at the end of a long lane on the side of a hill. As with so many holy places, there is an open space in front of the door where people can gather to greet one another, exchange news, and discuss their faith.

The synagogue is named after a rabbi who came here to write and pray. He died in 1572 and is buried nearby.

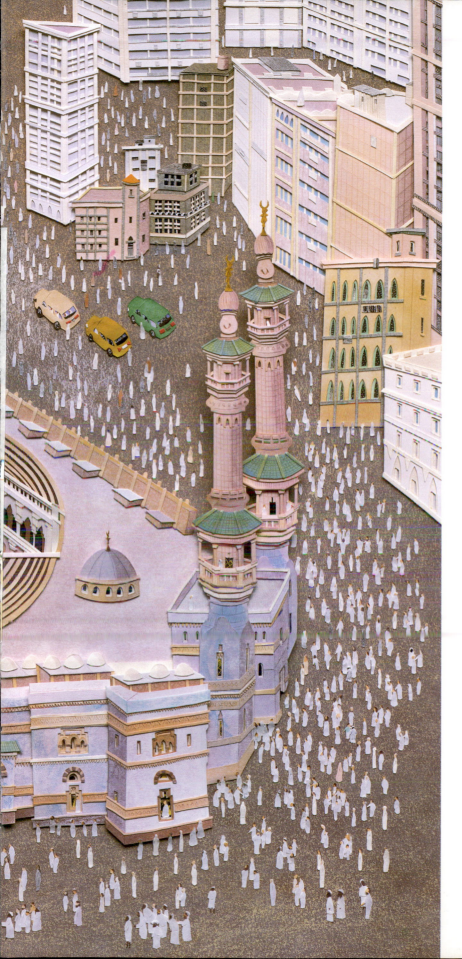

And people flock to this sacred place from around the world.

THE KAABA

Mecca, Saudi Arabia · Traditionally about 2000 B.C.E.

This is the holiest of Muslim sacred places. Muhammad believed that the Kaaba was built by Abraham and Ishmael.

The Kaaba is a simple stone building with a flat roof within the Grand Mosque. The building's covering, which is replaced each year, is a black cloth embroidered with verses from the Koran in silver and gold.

All Muslims face the Kaaba when they pray. If possible, they visit it at least once in their lifetime to walk around it seven times, kiss the black stone in the corner, and joyfully shout praises to God.

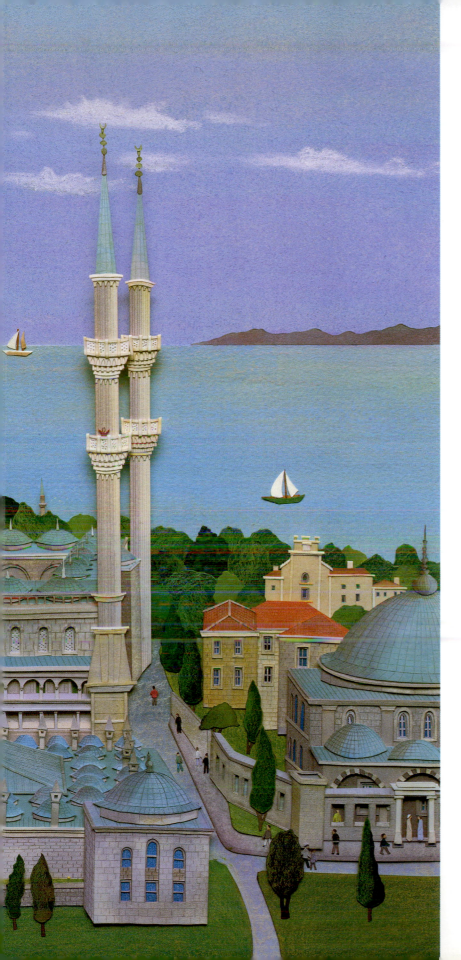

Sacred places
fill your heart
and echo your beliefs
as you pray quietly...

SULTAN AHMET MOSQUE
Istanbul, Turkey • 1609–1616

After Muhammad died, his followers worried that he and not the words of the Koran would be worshiped. This is why no images of Muhammad exist. Muslims also avoid the depiction of images of any living forms to guard against idolatry. Instead, mosques are decorated with elegantly written passages from the Koran and magnificent geometric patterns of carved stone, molded clay, or tile. The intricate tile work in the Sultan Ahmet Mosque is mostly blue, which is why it's often called the Blue Mosque.

or sing loudly
with a joyful voice!

CONCORD BAPTIST CHURCH

Boston, Massachusetts • 1869

In early America, many African slaves became Christians, and they developed their own way of praising the Lord. Lively and vibrant songs expressed their culture, opened their hearts, raised their spirits, and gave them hope. Their songs are the foundation of much American music.

This church's famous choir has performed around the country. But what they really love is singing with their own congregation with such enthusiasm that the walls seem to shake with joy.

And some
sacred places
aren't made
by people
at all.

SITES OF SACRED PLACES

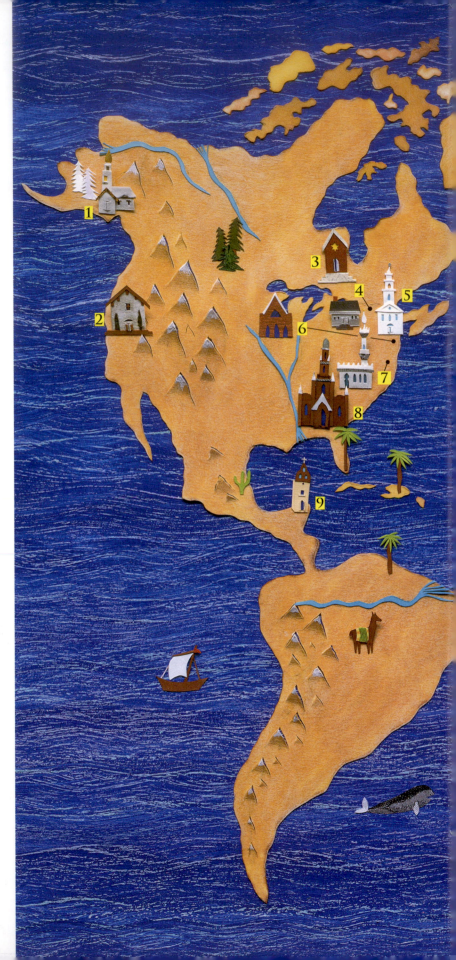

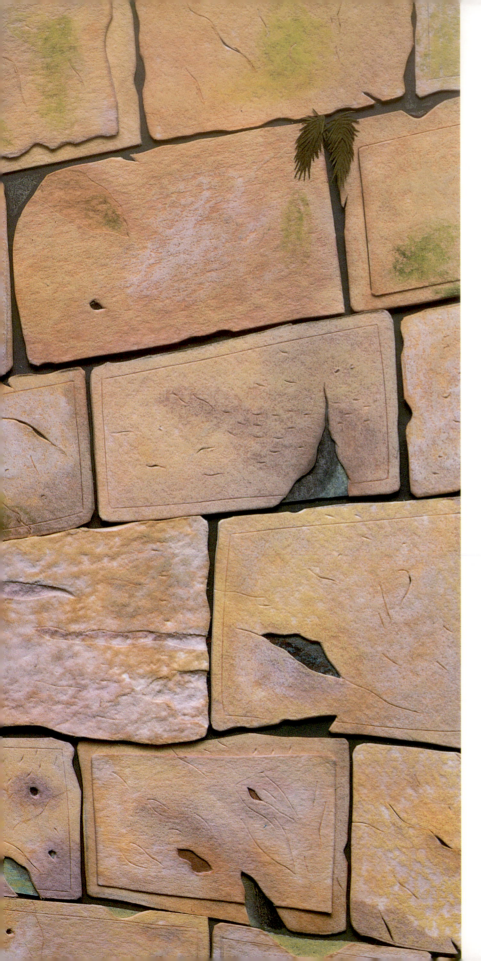

To the elder Philemons who spread the Word with enthusiasm, and to Allen, who made a joyful noise. —P.S.

To those who visit these places for peace. —G.L.

———⚹———

COVER

SHORE TEMPLE
Mahabalipuram, Tamil Nadu, India • About 700
 Perfect geometric shapes are considered by many to be sacred. These special shapes underlie most of the world's art and architecture. The design of this temple is based on a circle within a square within a "golden" rectangle.

TITLE PAGE IMAGES — RIGHT TO LEFT

ORIANNEBURGER STRASSE SYNAGOGUE
Berlin, Germany

IGLESIA DE LA VIRGEN DE LA CANDELARIA
Ticuch, Yucatan, Mexico

ISLAMIC CENTER
Washington, D.C.

KUMBUM—TEMPLE OF 100,000 BUDDHAS
Gyantse, Tibet

LAKSHMI NARAYAN TEMPLE
Delhi, India

ACKNOWLEDGEMENTS—We'd like to thank the Rev. Alexandra Honigsberg, Union Theological Seminary Church historian; Benjamin G. Zimmer; and Swordsmith Productions for their assistance with the text and insights into the faiths highlighted within these pages.

TEXT COPYRIGHT © 2000 by Philemon Sturges. Illustrations copyright © 2000 by Giles Laroche. All rights reserved. This book, or parts thereof, may not be reproduced in any form without permission in writing from the publisher, G. P. Putnam's Sons, a division of Penguin Putnam Books for Young Readers, 345 Hudson Street, New York, NY 10014. G. P. Putnam's Sons, Reg. U.S. Pat. & Tm. Off. Published simultaneously in Canada. Printed in Hong Kong by South China Printing Co. (1988) Ltd. Designed by Sharon Murray Jacobs. Text set in 11-point Bembo. The three-dimensional illustrations were created on a variety of paper surfaces through a combination of drawing, painting, and papercutting. Library of Congress Cataloging-in-Publication Data Sturges, Philemon. Sacred places / Philemon Sturges; illustrated by Giles Laroche. p. cm. Summary: Describes various types of space that are sacred to different religions, including churches, mosques, synagogues, temples, and other shrines. 1. Sacred space—Juvenile literature. 2. Shrines—Juvenile literature. 3. Religions—Juvenile literature. [1. Sacred space. 2. Shrines. 3. Religions.] I. Laroche, Giles, ill. II. Title. BL580.S78 2000 291.3'5—dc21 98-31086 CIP AC ISBN 0-399-23317-2 10 9 8 7 6 5 4 3 2 1 FIRST IMPRESSION